A NOTE TO PARENTS

Reading Aloud with Your Child

Research shows that reading books aloud is the single most valuable support parents can provide in helping children learn to read.

- Be a ham! The more enthusiasm you display, the more your child will enjoy the book.
- Run your finger underneath the words as you read to signal that the print carries the story.
- Leave time for examining the illustrations more closely; encourage your child to find things in the pictures.
- Invite your youngster to join in whenever there's a repeated phrase in the text.
- Link up events in the book with similar events in your child's life.
- If your child asks a question, stop and answer it. The book can be a means to learning more about your child's thoughts.

Listening to Your Child Read Aloud

The support of your attention and praise is absolutely crucial to your child's continuing efforts to learn to read.

- If your child is learning to read and asks for a word, give it immediately so that the meaning of the story is not interrupted. DO NOT ask your child to sound out the word.
- On the other hand, if your child initiates the act of sounding out, don't intervene.
- If your child is reading along and makes what is called a miscue, listen for the sense of the miscue. If the word "road" is substituted for the word "street," for instance, no meaning is lost. Don't stop the reading for a correction.
- If the miscue makes no sense (for example, "horse" for "house"), ask your child to reread the sentence because you're not sure you understand what's just been read.
- Above all else, enjoy your child's growing command of print and make sure you give lots of praise. *You are your child's first teacher—and the most important one. Praise from you is critical for further risk-taking and learning.*

—Priscilla Lynch
Ph.D., New York University
Educational Consultant

For Irving Sarnoff, M.D.
—for his many kinds of help
—R.B.G.

Special thanks to Bernard Ghelman, M.D., Department of Radiology, Hospital for Special Surgery, New York City, for reviewing the manuscript for this book.

Text copyright © 1978 by Ruth Belov Gross.
Illustrations copyright © 1994 by Steve Björkman.
All rights reserved. Published by Scholastic Inc.
HELLO READER! and CARTWHEEL BOOKS are registered trademarks
of Scholastic Inc.

Library of Congress Cataloging-in-Publication Data

Gross, Ruth Belov.
    A book about your skeleton / by Ruth Belov Gross ; illustrated by Steve Björkman.
        p.   cm. — (Hello reader! Level 4)
    ISBN 0-590-48312-9
    1. Skeleton—Juvenile literature.   2. Bones–Juvenile literature.
[1. Skeleton.   2. Bones.]   I. Björkman, Steve, ill.   II. Title.   III. Series.
QM101.G74   1994
611'.71—dc20   93-49824
                                                                                        CIP
                                                                                        AC

12 11 10 9 8 7 6 5 4   4 5 6 7 8 9/9
                              Printed in the U.S.A.   23
                   First Scholastic printing, October 1994

A Book About Your
SKELETON

by Ruth Belov Gross
Illustrated by Steve Björkman

Hello Reader!—Level 4

SCHOLASTIC INC.
Cartwheel B·O·O·K·S ®

New York   Toronto   London   Auckland   Sydney

Everybody has bones.
Everybody needs them.
If you didn't have any bones,
you would flop around like spaghetti.

Your bones are hard and stiff.
The rest of you is soft.
The hard, stiff bones
help hold the soft part up.
And they give the soft part a shape.

You can feel the hard, stiff bones
that help hold you up
and give your body its shape.

You have more than 200 bones
in your body — long bones,
short bones, flat bones,
curved bones, little bones,
big bones.

There are bones in your head
and bones in your toes
and bones almost everywhere else
in between.

All of your bones put together
are your skeleton.

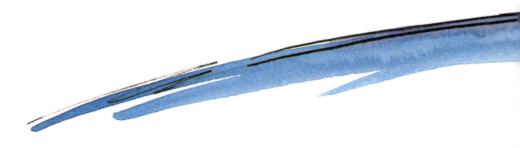

But a skeleton isn't just
a pile of bones.

This isn't a skeleton.

Neither is this.

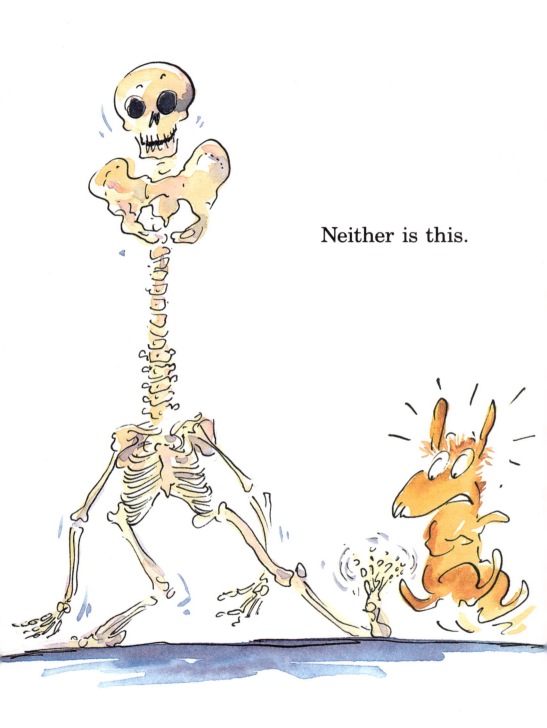

The bones have to be
put together right!

It's a good thing
that bones are hard.
If you bumped your head,
you might get a headache.
But the soft squashy brain
inside your head
would be safe.
Your head bones are
like a hard hat.
They keep your brain
from getting hurt.

The bones in your head
are your skull bones.
Construction workers
have to be extra careful.
So they wear hard hats
over their hard skulls.

Your heart and lungs are soft and
squashy too.
But nothing will happen to them —
even when somebody hugs you
too tight.

The bones that curve around your chest
keep your heart and lungs from getting hurt.

The bones that curve
around your chest
are your ribs.
You can feel them
under your skin.
Maybe you can even
count them.

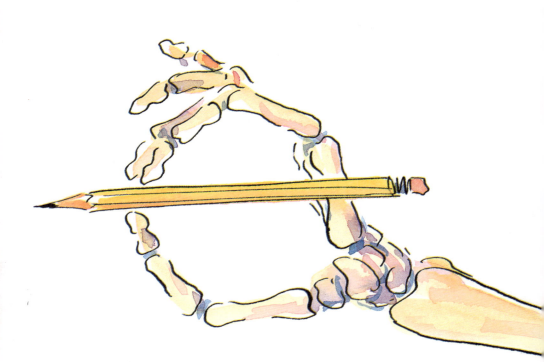

Every bone in your body
is joined to at least one other bone.

Put your thumb and first finger together.
Can you see where your fingers bend?

The bending places are where
two bones are joined.
The bending places are joints.

Strong, stretchy bands, like big rubber bands,
hold the bones together.
These bands are called ligaments.

Without the joints in your fingers,
your fingers would stick straight out.
You could never play ball
or play the piano
or button your buttons
or peel a banana.

Shoulders, elbows, and wrists are joints.
So are hips and ankles and knees.
How many things can you think of
that these joints help you do?

Other joints in other parts of your body
also help you move.

You can twist and turn and touch your toes
because you have joints in your backbone.

Your backbone is made of many little bones called vertebrae.

Another name for backbone is spine.

You can open and close your mouth
because you have two important joints
in your skull.
Put your fingers in front of your ears
to feel them.

There are other places in your skull
where bones are joined —
but these joints do not move.

Your bones help you move.
And your joints help you move.
But you couldn't move —
you couldn't even stand —
if you didn't have muscles too.

Your muscles make your bones move.
The muscles are attached to your bones.
They pull on the bones to move them.

It takes many muscles
just to take one step —
or to wiggle one of your toes.

Your skeleton began growing
before you were born.
It wasn't hard and bony then.
It was made of soft, rubbery cartilage.
If you want to know
what cartilage feels like,
pinch the end of your nose,
or bend your ear.

This baby's bones
are still soft and rubbery.

Bit by bit, your skeleton got a little harder.
Bone began to take the place
of the soft cartilage.

After you were born, your bones
kept on getting harder.
There was less and less cartilage in them.

Your bones are getting harder all the time.
And they are getting bigger too.
Your growing bones
are helping to make you bigger and taller.
They will keep on growing until
bone has replaced almost all of the cartilage.

Even an adult has some cartilage —
at the ends of some bones,
in the ears and nose,
and in a few other places.

Some of the things you eat
help your growing bones
get harder and stronger.

How old will you be
when you stop growing?
That's hard to say.
Most likely the bones in your legs
will keep on growing
and making you taller
until you are somewhere
between 14 and 18.

Your arm bones
will stop growing
at about the same time
as your leg bones.

But your hands and
your feet may grow
for another year or two.

Most girls stop growing
before most boys do,
but almost everyone
finishes all of their growing
by the time they are 19 or 20.

When your bones are fully grown,
they will be stronger than granite rock.
But even though bones are strong,
bones can break.

What happens if you break a bone
in your leg?
The doctor puts the broken parts together,
and you get a plaster cast to wear.
You can ask your friends to sign the cast.
Then you wait for the bone to heal.

The cast keeps the broken bone
from jiggling around.
The bone will mend itself.

An X-ray picture will show the doctor
how well the bone is healing.

No matter how big or how small
a bone is,
and no matter how it is shaped,
there are spaces inside the bone.

The big, long bones
in your arms and your legs
have big, long spaces inside them.

This is what the inside
of a leg bone looks like.

Blood cells are made
at both ends of the bone.

Blood cells are made here too —
but only while you are growing.

And at the ends of these bones
there are tiny spaces,
like the spaces in a sponge.
Other bones have tiny spaces too.
The spaces are filled with a mushy material
called bone marrow.
Red bone marrow
is where blood cells are made.

So your bones do more than hold you up
and help you move
and give your body a shape
and protect your squashy insides.
Your bones also help make your blood.

There are 206 bones in a human skeleton.
Every bone has a name.

In a real skeleton, the bones are white.
The bones in this picture, though,
have different colors, to make it easier
to tell them apart.

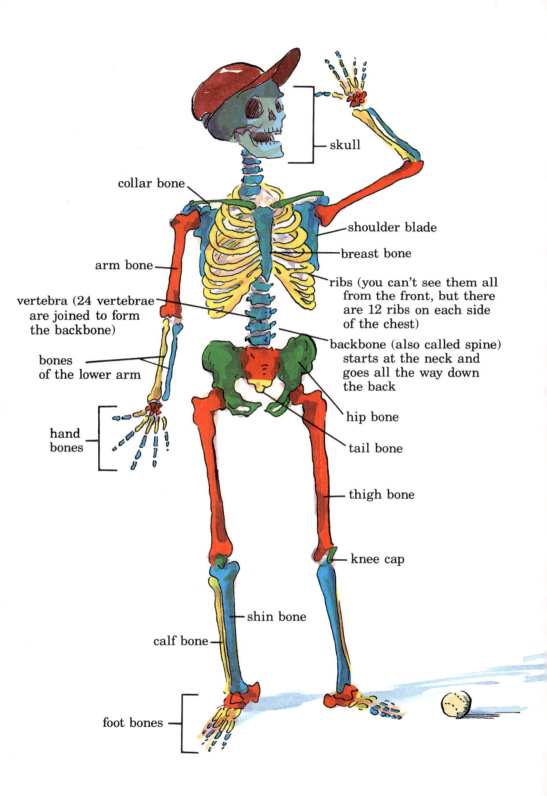

skull

collar bone

shoulder blade

breast bone

arm bone

ribs (you can't see them all
from the front, but there
are 12 ribs on each side
of the chest)

vertebra (24 vertebrae
are joined to form
the backbone)

backbone (also called spine)
starts at the neck and
goes all the way down
the back

bones
of the lower arm

hip bone

tail bone

hand
bones

thigh bone

knee cap

shin bone

calf bone

foot bones

These are the same bones with their scientific names.

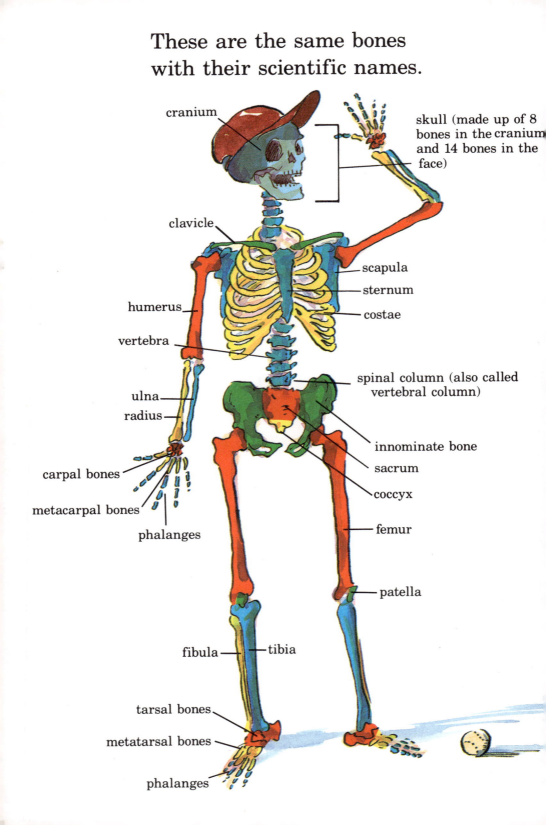

cranium

skull (made up of 8 bones in the cranium and 14 bones in the face)

clavicle

scapula

sternum

humerus

costae

vertebra

spinal column (also called vertebral column)

ulna

radius

innominate bone

sacrum

carpal bones

coccyx

metacarpal bones

femur

phalanges

patella

fibula — tibia

tarsal bones

metatarsal bones

phalanges